40 STUDIES FOR CLARINET

C. ROSE

Book I

Published in 2019 by Allegro Editions

40 Studies for Clarinet [1]
ISBN: 978-1-9748-9950-0 (paperback)

Cover design by Kaitlyn Whitaker

Cover image: "Close Up Detail of a Woodwind Clarinet"
by Mark Yuill, courtesy of Shutterstock;
"Music Sheet" by Danielo, courtesy of Shutterstock

ALLEGRO
EDITIONS

40 STUDIES
for
CLARINET.

BOOK I.

arr. by C. ROSE

7

21

www.ingramcontent.com/pod-product-compliance
Lightning Source LLC
Chambersburg PA
CBHW081357040426
42451CB00017B/3485